Never Stop Learning and growing!

Cn Sa

Release That Book & Get Paid

7 Core Marketing Strategies for Authors Who Want to Make Money from Books

Ari Squires

"Award-Winning Author of 10 Books"
Has Earned $350,000+ from One Book
CEO of SheEO Publishing Company

Release That Book & Get Paid:
7 Core Marketing Strategies for Authors Who Want to Make Money from Books
Ari Squires

Editing, Cover and Interior Design: SheEO Publishing Co
www.SheEOPublishing.com

First Printing 2018

ISBN #: 978-1-7335046-0-7

Disclaimer: The strategies provided in this book are personal growth recommendations and are not designed to substitute good judgment applicable to individual circumstances. The samples and examples are hypothetical and should not be taken as literal.

Published in the United States

Special FREE Bonus Gift for YOU!

To help you achieve more success, there are
FREE BONUS RESOURCES for you at:

www.FreeGiftFromAri.com

Get your 3 FREE in-depth training programs sharing how to create marketing magic, kick-start your business for under $50 without using social media, and attract more profits!

www.AriSquires.com

Additional Resources

#1 Offline Marketing Machine

Home Study Course

Winning secrets to get highly paid from your books, programs and services offline.

#2 Live Event Success Blueprint

Pack, Promote & Profit

Learn behind the scene secrets of how to make five and six figures from your live events.

www.AriSquires.com

Ari Squires

For your next event

For strong training programs that work for audiences of all types book Ari Squires for your next seminar, workshop, mastermind, or team training. Mrs. Squires has proven training techniques to increase your company's productivity and profits within a quarter of implementation.

FOR PRIVATE COACHING PLEASE CONTACT

Melanie Boothe
info@AriSquires.com
(540) 812-2770

(--Serious Inquiries Only--)

Visit www.AriSquires.com for booking

WHAT OTHERS ARE SAYING...

"Brava, Ari! This project is so well done."

-Abiola Abrams

When entrepreneur Ari Squires decided to create a film, she went in the right direction. Her *No More Chains* documentary is a testament to brave, authentic storytelling. The women of color in this project have been through it all—and are still standing. With this film, Ari Squires joins Hollywood media-makers such as Oprah Winfrey, Shonda Rhimes, Ava DuVernay and Issa Rae who have taken back our stories.

-Abiola Abrams: Author, Speaker, Spiritpreneur Coach & Self-Worth Revolutionary! Empowering Women Leaders to Live Out Loud

> **"Ari will be a part of the change we need right now."**
>
> -Isaiah Washington

-Isaiah Washington: Actor, "*Grey's Anatomy*", "*Exit Wounds*", "*Crooklyn*", "*Get on the Bus*", "*The 100*". NAACP Image Award Winner. Screen Actors Guild Awardee. Named as one of People's "50 Beautiful People"

> **"I had the most amazing time at Ari's Release The Chains Revenue Retreat. She knows how to gather groups of dynamic entrepreneurs."**
>
> -Kevin Harrington

-Kevin Harrington: Original Shark on the Hit TV Show, *Shark Tank*. Inventor of the Infomercial. $4 Billion in Sales on TV

> **"Ari knows how to lead and great leaders build great people."**
>
> -Paul C. Brunson

Ari knows how to win. I speak at a lot of events and this is the most welcome I have ever felt. Her team was hand-picked by her and ready to serve. You can tell who is a good leader by looking at their support team and tribe. Ari proves over and over again that she can move people into excellence. I'm always thrilled to work with her and call her my friend.

-Paul C. Brunson: USA Today Columnist. TV Host. Recognized internationally as one of the most successful matchmakers and small business leaders.

◆

CASE STUDIES

Being a part of Ari's tutelage and PUSH Mastermind group has helped me increase my businesses visibility and clientele just by applying key recommendations taught by her over the past three months.

Gigi McMillian, Kamisol Style Consultancy

I've made more money working with Ari in one month than I have my entire six years in business. She is nothing but a blessing!

Stephanie McNeal-Brown, Founder of Heartbreak to Happy Forgiveness Coaching

I began coaching with Ari in late 2015, At that time I only had 2 JumpStarz classes per week and 3 staff. As of October 2018, I'm averaging 15 classes a week, I have over 20 staff and I am a full-time entrepreneur because the income I make from JumpStarz allowed me to ditch my 9-5!
That's not it! I took all that I learned and started another business as well as helped my daughter launch Mari's Mailbox Post Painting. Coaching with Ari was the best investment I've ever made in myself. My confidence level, goals, and mindset has totally shifted. (so did my deposits to the bank). Ari definitely knows her shhhhh.

Patricia Clement, CEO JumpStarz

My goal before working with Ari as my business coach was to have consecutive $5k+ months. I am happy to announce that over the past six months I have done just that and October 2018 (exactly one year after working with Ari) I had my FIRST $13k month!!!
Other than the multitude of expert business strategies I've received from Ari what stands out the most is how she's helped build my confidence and that has made me become mentally stronger and believing more in myself.
I knew after making $13,000 from my first live event with Ari's assistance 8 months ago...I made the right decision to invest in myself.

Meisha Pigford, CEO Dream Celebrations

I hired Ari just wanting to be a good makeup artist, but after working with her I went from having zero customers at first to being completely booked up through the spring and summer. With the help of her amazing coaching services and mastermind group I am now able to have multiple revenue sources through my business, increased clientele, and endless network of business professionals, and the confidence and know how to make my business a six-figure business.

Shavon Dotson, Flawless Faces by Shavon

Ari's guidance with our non-profit organization has been beyond words. She has helped us get a clear vision for our organizational goals and has helped us raise money for our youth programs. I highly recommend her because she understands business and cares about the success of others so deeply it oozes out her pores.

James Jackson, Co-founder TOPKATS Group

💰 *I had never heard of a business coach until I went to Ari's Release The Chains event. I am so glad I did! I see my business as a business now after working with Ari as my new partner in business (business coach). She has helped me create budgets and realistic profit goals that are growing my business and helping me stand out.*

Kendra King, ASIS Employee Training

💰 *My Travel retreats were not selling out until I started working with Ari. If it wasn't for her coaching and guidance my business would not have come this far.*

Faye Brown, Cater2UTravels, LLC

◆

FOREWORD

You may remember me from being featured on the hit ABC TV show, "Secret Millionaire." If you do not know of the show, here is the basic premise from show promotions:

"What happens when business motivational speaker and self-made millionaire James Malinchak is picked up by an ABC television crew, placed on an airplane with no money, credit cards, cell phone, laptop or watch, and is whisked off to an impoverished neighborhood, where he had to survive on $44.66 cents for a week?

The show features Malinchak leaving his current lifestyle in search of real-life heroes who are making a difference in their local community. He ultimately reveals himself as a millionaire and rewards them with a portion of his own money to further their cause by gifting them with checks of his own money totaling over $100,000. If you watched ABC's 'Secret Millionaire' you know that James is no ordinary entrepreneur. He is a self-made millionaire with a strong passion for giving back and serving others."

Amazingly, over 10 MIILLION people watched me on the show! Whether I am speaking at a conference, walking through an airport, consulting for an entrepreneur or just hanging out at a coffee shop, I always seem to get asked the same question. "What was it like being on Secret

Millionaire when you had to live undercover in an impoverished neighborhood and how did it affect you?"

My answer is always the same.

The greatest gift you can have is when you simply give in order to help and serve others. There is no better feeling than when you know you have made a positive difference in lives of others.

And that is exactly what my friend **Ari Squires** and her teachings can do for you! She will inspire you through sharing her wisdom and personal experiences.

Ari is an author, speaker and leader who truly cares about making a positive difference in the lives of others.

In this book you will be inspired by her genuine, caring nature for making a difference in your life. And her strategies can help you to achieve more than ever before.

Some strategies may comfort you while others may challenge your old paradigm. One thing is for certain. Ari and her strategies will stamp your spirit with an abundance of love, hope and encouragement so you can reach new levels of courage, fulfillment and personal happiness.

It is my sincere honor to introduce to you Ari and her amazing book!

-James Malinchak
Featured on ABCs Hit TV Show, "Secret Millionaire"
Authored 20 Books, Delivered 3,000 Presentations
& 1,000 Consultations
Best-Selling Author, *Millionaire Success Secrets*
Founder, www.MillionaireFreeBook.com

HERE'S WHAT'S INSIDE

◆

INTRODUCTION

Plenty of people have what it takes to write a book, but not all of them know how to market their books – and themselves – for success. Do you want to learn how to turn your book into a moneymaker? If so, this guide is for you. I'm going to teach you how to complete and market your best book, and I'll be answering some of the most frequently asked questions I receive from new authors.

You may already have a basic understanding of some of the concepts I'm going to cover. You'll also find that what works for one author or book doesn't necessarily work for another. As a business coach who helps entrepreneurs plan for profits, and the CEO of a publishing company, I've learned the insider secrets that writers are dying to know: namely, how to market their books in order to get paid. After finding my own path to success, I've been lucky enough to be able to teach my clients to do the same. Now I'm going to teach you, too.

WHY SHOULD YOU LISTEN TO ME?

My name is Ari Squires and I have been an entrepreneur since elementary school.

I am a best-selling award-winning author of ten books. I'm also the head of SheEO Publishing, where we offer writing, editing, publishing, graphic design and production services. I've directed and produced two films, *No More Chains*, and *No More Chains 2: It's Time For Change*, which are inspired by my very first book, *Release the Chains – A Woman's Roadmap for Finding the Strength to Reclaim Her Destiny.* This book was where I first shared my story: I was a young woman with low self-worth, getting into trouble with the law, but I knew that there was more for me. I was able to discover my purpose within the jail cell.

When I was released, I knew that I wanted to inspire women and girls to fulfill their potential, even though I wasn't living up to my own at the time. I wanted to inspire them to grow, to be their best selves and to do what they want to do in life. You know – go after your dreams, full speed ahead, don't let anything stop you! When I listened to the stories of the women who were incarcerated with me, I realized that they all had something in common: mentally, emotionally or generationally, each was standing in the way of her own success. Sure, some things are beyond our control, but that doesn't make us powerless. Each of us has the power to succeed against all odds, overcoming anything that's stacked against us.

Before I wrote *Release the Chains*, I owned and operated a performing arts school for ten years. I was giving back to the community, mentoring girls and working with a non-profit organization called Lend-a-Hand, Uplift-a-Child, Foundation. But I had never shared my story, so I felt like I wasn't being truthful. I felt kind of fake.

Once I decided to share my story, I created a whole movement. My first book has garnered over $350,000 and counting. You can do it, too! In this guide, **I'm going to share tips on how to leverage your book into business opportunities.** You can use your book to start movements, to get you on television, to sell your products or services and to grow your business.

WHAT THIS BOOK COVERS

Maybe you are already an author, looking to re-launch an existing book or start another. Maybe you're about to publish your first book. Maybe you just have an idea, and you're reading because you want to know how to do it *right* from start to finish. No matter where you're coming from, I can help you market your book – and yourself – for success. First, you have to know your *why*; the reason you are writing, in order to hone in on your target audience. You have to format your book, inside and out, so that it will position you for success; assembling a team of professionals or working with a business coach can help you stay on track and build a personal brand. Most of all, you need a marketing plan that creates anticipation before you release your book and continues to engage readers after your launch date. This will allow you to leverage your book to create additional income streams.

Would you launch a business without putting together a business plan? Of course not! I've seen too many people launch their books without a plan. It can seem overwhelming at first, but the trick is to build and market the best book for you. Now, the key word is *you.* Not every suggestion in this guide will be for you. I'll be going over several different marketing strategies that may or may not work for you. It's okay to just take what you need and make it work for you.

You may be thinking, "this is too much, Ari, I can't do it all," but it's okay: you don't have to! Sometimes we need additional guidance, and I'm here to help you to figure out what's right for you and your book. **Trust me, by the time you reach the end of this guide, you're going to know how to market your own like a pro!** Best of all, you can learn from anywhere… even the comfort of your own home, in your pajamas.

The first secret that I learned about becoming a published author is this: it's about list-building. **Your book is your product *and* your business card; it's the gateway to creating a tribe of people who will eventually want to buy something a lot more expensive than a $20.00 book from you.**

◆

PRE-LAUNCH BUZZ

START WITH YOUR WHY

Why do people write books?

Some people write to educate or inform. Non-fiction books, news articles and technical documents all serve this purpose. Some people aim to entertain – think of your favorite summer vacation novel or juicy gossip tell-all rag. Some writers share riveting tales; thrillers, romances and autobiographies captivate readers with poetic language and imagery. Inspiring and motivating others to make changes in their lifestyles, businesses or habits is another big one right now, and falls in the self-help or personal development field.

These reasons also tie into why we read books. Some read to escape; others search for solutions to problems. Sadly, only ten percent of people who buy books actually get through the first chapter. This is why I am passionate about teaching my clients leverage: truth is, no one is really reading the book. Sorry to burst your bubble.

All it takes to become a writer is to write, but what I want you to understand is that it takes more than just good writing to become a successful author. Becoming an author is about starting a business, and that's what I want to focus on in this guide. **Anybody can sell a book for $20.00. I'm more interested in talking about real money, real leverage, real marketing strategies and tactics that you can incorporate into your strategy to receive enormous, six and seven-figure results.** As long as you're willing to put in the effort, you can build an empire from your books.

The first thing you have to do is focus on your *why.* Why are you writing? Open up your laptop or get out a pen and paper, and brainstorm as much as you can, even if it's all over the place at first. Extend this to your new business venture: what is your ultimate business goal? You'll want to think carefully about both your topic and your business objective. It's okay if they are tangentially related – everything will come together soon.

How much money do you want to make? How many books do you want to sell? What do you want your book to do for you? Who could benefit from your specific set of skills and experience? By the end of this guide, you will have the answer.

We all want to inspire, to motivate, and to share our stories with a community. Whether you've been meaning to write a book forever but have been putting it off, or it's the next step in promoting yourself as an expert speaker, consultant, or coach in your field, it's essential to create a plan. Every book I've written has had a different business goal, but they all have one thing in common: all of them have to do with creating a new revenue stream or supporting a coaching or consulting program that generates revenue.

THE BIRTH OF A MOVEMENT: CREATING ANTICIPATION

Actionable goals are easier to achieve than loosely-defined big-picture ideas. It takes consistency and hard work on your part, but it also requires that you plant the seed that gets people talking. No matter where you're at in the writing or publishing process, it's never too early to generate some hype around your book.

Seeding means letting your audience know what you're working on. Using social media is a great way to reach out to your community, whether it's your target audience or just friends and family who will help you get started. The sooner you start seeding the book, the better – it doesn't need to be finished in order to get people interested.

One of my coaching clients, Theresa made me exceptionally proud when she posted this on her social media timeline, "I'm so proud of myself, last night I finished chapter 3 of my book, I can't wait to send my draft over to the publisher." That's seeding, that's piquing people's interest, that's getting people excited about your work.

When I was working on my last book, *The Mindset of a CEO: Seven Core Principles of Sustaining Profitable Success as a Woman in Business,* I held a webinar based on just the first few chapters. This allowed me to generate interest and sales when the book came out. It also helped me to learn about my audience and tailor the project specifically to their needs. Again, I wasn't looking at how much money I was going to make. Sure, it's great to be able to make a few hundred dollars in sales at a speaking engagement, but I am always thinking of the bigger picture: how can I turn what I already have into something more?

With *Release That Book and Get Paid*, I took it a step further. I've been using this book to make money **since before it was written!** This time, the webinar was central to the pre-launch marketing strategy. Because I've outlined a clear *why* and created anticipation in my community, I've had readers, clients and followers asking, "when is the book coming out?" and it keeps me motivated knowing that my book is already in demand.

Novelty and excitement are commodities, and everyone wants the latest and greatest, whether it's in fashion or the entertainment industry or beyond. As a marketer and business owner, you want people to anticipate what's coming. The opening of my film, *No More Chains*, sold out before we even finished post-production. We were receiving media inquiries even though we hadn't sent out press releases yet. That's because I created a marketing campaign that has awakened excitement in my community and beyond.

Seed, seed, seed! Even if it's just an idea, you have to put it out there. There are as many ways to do this as there are authors – the possibilities are endless, but you won't get your community excited about your book ahead of time if you don't tell anyone about it. Here are some things you can do to spread the word:

- **Guest appearances –** local TV programs, radio stations, podcasts, news outlets, and blog posts can be great platforms to unveil your plan.
- **Courses, webinars and conferences -** free and paid teleclasses, webinars, and events related to your field.
- **Build a web presence –** in addition to your own personal website, you can set up "splash pages" that provide information about individual projects. Social media is more important and more useful than ever!
- **Come up with a catchy title –** even if it's just a working title, giving your book a name helps you think of it as a "real" book, and it prompts people to ask questions.

If you wait until you've finished writing to put your book to work for you, you'll miss out on opportunities to make money, connect with prospective clients and grow your business. You have to create excitement, and you have to create a marketing strategy that works for you. **If you're considering becoming an Amazon Best-Seller, know that it takes a pre-launch campaign to succeed**. This means thinking ahead. It takes strategy to sell books – or any products and services, for that matter. Building a strategy takes time, and it's not one-size-fits-all. All of these ideas have been successful for me and my clients, but not every idea is right for every project. **Planning is critical, but at the end of the day, it's about a bigger *why*.** It's up to you to know what that *why* is even before you start writing.

The strategic planning that goes on behind-the-scenes before you even launch your book will help you to understand who you are trying to reach, why you are writing, and how you can engage with your community of readers. Your book should create a movement. A movement can be anything. It can be a new business; it can be growth in your community; it can be a new career, partnership or affiliate; whatever your movement will be is up to you. Your movement doesn't have to be the same as my movement, and vice versa.

Start marketing while you're still writing. You have to plant and water the seed if you want it to grow.

◆

IDENTIFY YOUR AUDIENCE

You already know your book is going to be great: you're sharing your story, motivating people and growing a business. When I wrote my first book, it was amazing to hear the fantastic feedback from my community. Not only did I grow as a person, I developed professionally, too; positioning myself as an expert, taking on new clients and launching a conference. All of these things were possible because I knew *why* – and who – I was writing for.

They say "it takes a village," but I think "community" is a stronger word. To me, a village seems spread out; a village shares a geographic location, but not necessarily an attitude. Not every village is a community. To be a part of a community means to be a part of something bigger than oneself, actively participating and lifting others up. Communities have the power to influence and inspire. It takes strategy and finesse, but as an author, you'll have to learn to create a community based in the audience you're writing for.

THE IDEAL AUDIENCE

Who do you want to work with? Whose work do you admire? Who needs your help? That's your ideal audience. As long as your book speaks to the core of your ideal audience – helping them identify and solve a problem – you will automatically attract them. This means less work on marketing yourself and more time spent on growing your business!

To be successful in any profession, you have to create an ideal client profile. As a business coach, I consult with about four to five people a week and far too many of them have never put together an ideal client profile. How can you speak to your audience if you don't know who they are? **In order to speak to the core of your audience, you need to know them from top to bottom.**

Here are some things to consider when thinking about your ideal client:

- **Demographics** – is your ideal client a man or a woman? How old are they? What do they look like?

- **Family** – are they single, married, widowed or divorced? How many children do they have? Are they stay-at-home-moms or caring for elderly parents?

- **Location** – where do they live?

- **Profession** – are they professionals? Entrepreneurs? *What is their income?* If you're targeting your brand to organizations, are they million-dollar companies or six-figure local businesses? You need to be sure that your target audience can afford your products and services.

- **Values** – what do they value? Family, children, spirituality?

- **Personality** – what do they enjoy doing? Sports, community service, shopping?

I know exactly who my ideal client is: what they look like, how much money they make, how many children they have and more. I can tell you who my ideal client is because I know how I can help them. **Usually, our ideal clients are very similar to us; they've probably been through some of the same things that we've been through and faced similar challenges.** The most important thing to ask yourself about your ideal client is ***what are their challenges***? Then, use the answer to that question to identify how you – and your book – can provide a solution.

Here's an example: when I was a little girl, my mom used to make us wash the floors with a little sponge and big old white mop. I hated the nasty grey water and having to wring the dirty mop out. When the battery-operated Swiffer came out, all I had to do was sweep and press a little button – that finally solved my problem!

I never thought of it as a problem, just another status-quo chore that I had to deal with. Sure, it was a challenge, but I hadn't realized it was a problem that could be solved until somebody created a solution. That's how you have to think of your book, your services, your story and brand. How are you the answer to somebody's prayers?

TALK THE TALK

Home Depot wouldn't be successful if they didn't know their market. Walmart wouldn't be successful if they didn't have a clear picture of who their ideal clients are. Big companies, mid-size companies and successful entrepreneurs know it's all about language. When you take a closer look at their marketing materials and strategies, you'll see that good copywriting is just as important as good long-form writing. "Copy" here doesn't mean to imitate; copy is the written material that gets your message out. Whether you use social media pages, websites, print ads or other forms, you have to learn how to best reach your ideal audience.

For me, this comes kind of naturally because I have the gift of gab, but when it comes to launching a business, you have to be strategic. Always pay attention to what you're saying (and how you're saying it), keeping your ideal client in mind at all times.

Since I've identified and experienced the struggles that my ideal clients are facing, I know what to say to them – and what not to say. I can speak to their core and relate to them without insulting them. Your audience should feel empowered by your messaging.

Here's another example: the Push Planner®. I used to write important info on sticky notes, which was handy when I first wrote it down, but afterwards I would frequently lose or misplace the notes. Once, I realized I had thrown a sticky note away and thought, "Man, that was a good contact! That could have turned into a client. I just lost out on an opportunity. I threw away some money because I wrote his number on a sticky note."

That was a turning point for me. I developed the Push Planner®, a sales, profit and financial business planner for entrepreneurs, so that I could put everything in one place: contacts, notes, connections, weekly follow-ups.

Since I've already "been there, done that," I know that there's nothing else like it on the market. Plus, I know how to say the right things in order to get a "yes" from an interested prospect. My ideal client has been in the same position I used to be in once or twice before, writing something on a scrap of paper or the back of a business card and then not being able to find it. They didn't realize that they needed the Push Planner® until I asked the right questions, like, "aren't you tired of losing track of things?"

Do you see how I spoke to the core of their challenge? If I wouldn't have said what I said, they would not have realized it was a problem or that it could be solved! My clients and I can relate to each other, and they are inclined to check out my products and services.

If you're speaking to the core of your audience in your marketing copy, you won't be so frustrated wondering, "what's going on? I'm doing all my social media posts, I'm doing what everybody else is doing, I'm being consistent, etc., why aren't people buying my book?". If you're not speaking to the core of the reader by showing them how you can solve a problem, then no one is going to be interested. You've got to create something that people will want to buy. It's easy once you know what problem your target audience needs solved.

Q&A: HOW DO I START?

I recently retired from the Army. I want to position myself as an expert in areas that I'm passionate and knowledgeable about while creating a new stream of income. How do you get clear about the core?

The simplest way is to follow my advice and create an ideal client profile. You can't run a successful business without it, no matter the size. If you've never created an ideal client profile, spend an hour brainstorming. You can even use yourself as an example.

What about different target audiences? I feel like I have two different audiences; how do I keep them separate?

You can't. Your book should only have one audience. If not, you're going to confuse both. They won't know for sure if they should buy or not, because they're not sure if you can help them. Each book should have one target audience.

My primary target audience is black women between 35 and 55, but I also work with older white gentlemen in their 60's and 70's. They want to hire me because I'm still speaking to their core. When you think about your ideal client, remember that they're just that – ideal. Of course you're going to attract readers from other demographics, but you've got to remember to speak to your target audience first and foremost.

If you have two different target audiences, stick to one

at a time until you get things up and running, then move to the others. For a long time, I was focused exclusively on my coaching business, which I marketed like crazy. I went to events I wrote books, I did everything. Once the business was doing well, people started to recognize me for it and I had a steady income. That was when I finally launched SheEO Publishing, which I was running on the back end. During the first year I made $35,000, but the second year I did over six figures in business. Since I was working behind-the-scenes, I didn't put the word out for about eighteen months, and few people knew about it. That was because I had to focus on one audience at a time. I needed people to know me for something. Once they did, I merged the two and then it became the same audience.

What are the most important aspects to cover when establishing your ideal client profile?

If you only have time to focus on a few components, make it these five:

- Gender
- Income
- Education
- What their key challenges are
- How you can help

BE A LEADER, NOT A FOLLOWER

As you know, a book can start a movement. A movement happens when a community or a tribe gets behind you, supporting you and cooperating with you. You'll find that your community is made up of readers who want to buy your products and utilize your services. For some people, it happens very quickly, but for others, it takes a little bit more time to build. It depends on your target audience and how aggressively you market to them.

Hopefully, you are learning how to create sources of income from your tribe or community; they're buying your books and consulting with you, and things like that. It can be a lengthy process, and sometimes it takes a little bit of investment to get it done. If you're going to pay to buy in to a community, make sure that it's the right community. These days, people are buying likes and followers on social media. You can pay to have your pages built by the pros, and even buy analytic software to gauge who's engaged and who is not. If you're going to go this route, continue to engage with your readers and continue to be yourself. It's the best way to increase traffic.

When you start a movement, you're moving people to take action. This is part of my personal *why*; I don't care if anybody buys my book or not, but I want people to take action in their own lives. My movement is "No More Chains," and whether somebody follows me or not, I want them to feel empowered. I want them to release their chains, and I want my life story to show them that it's possible; they can live a life that they love or create a business that they are passionate about just as I have. I want them to move to support a bigger cause, a greater good, a brighter future, whatever it may be. I want the authors who work with me to be successful.. I want my clients to engage with their communities and each other in order to create new businesses and opportunities. What type of action do you want people to take by watching you from your book, from your product, your ministry?

Many of my book publishing clients are ministers and pastors. They want to bring people closer to Jesus Christ – that's the movement they want to inspire. So how do we do that? We have to share the story of how they got closer to the Lord so that readers can relate to where you were and get inspired by where you are now.

Some people aren't worried about movement, but they should be: movements create change; create inspiration; create profits; create action; create ministries; create change in our youths. Think about former First Lady Michelle Obama's public health campaign, Let's Move!, which helped bring gardens to inner city schools and encouraged kids to exercise. It's amazing what a movement can do to benefit a community, and no movement or community is too small to do some good.

Maybe you're putting out a new brand or delving into a new niche. For example, my film *No More Chains* fits a new niche: inspirational entertainment. It's more theatrical than the work I normally do, but it's still a niche interest. I've kept my original audience, but now I'm attracting more men.

Your book and your movement is a destiny of sorts. It's your purpose for writing, so you want to make sure that your audience is on board with your movement. This takes some strategizing.

My "No More Chains" movement aims to empower people to win. What is your movement going to be? Here are some ideas from the authors I've worked with:

My movement is for women to be purpose-driven. I want to inspire, empower, and motivate women to unwrap their gifts so they can walk in their purpose. - **Taneta**

I want to inspire women to create lives of love on purpose. I want to help people to see the power of grace and know how powerful they are. – **Sherika**

My movement, I think is to inspire young girls and women to live their truth out loud. To own it shamelessly and to learn what it really means to live aimlessly. – **Ingrid**

My movement is to empower and inspire people to live again after setbacks and keep the faith that they can make it. – **Anita**

My mission: girls who dream become women with vision. I want to encourage teen moms to dream big and live intentionally. – **Ida**

My motto is "freedom is who you are and what you create." I want to inspire people to think outside the box and pursue their dreams. – Natasha

Whether you're writing to further an existing profession, or you're looking to launch a career as a full-time author, it's safe to bet you're writing because you're passionate about your subject matter. Someone out there is waiting for you to show up with your movement, with your messages and with your mission, with your purpose, with your smile, with your tenacity, with your determination, with your gifts. Let this movement fuel you!

Your movement says a lot about you: this is what people need to see, hear, read and feel in order to feel connected to you. **This human connection is the most important thing you can develop and leverage to release your book and get paid.**

◆

ASSEMBLE YOUR TEAM & WRITE YOUR BOOK

Think of all the books you've ever started but didn't finish. Whether you gave it up because the subject matter was confusing or the format was not engaging, you're not alone: based on data from Amazon and Kobo, about three-quarters of the readers who purchase best-selling titles **never read them cover-to-cover.**

It's not uncommon to flip through a book, picking and choosing what you want to focus on. I was taught to speed read when I was in the eighth grade, and since then I've picked up my fair share of books to just get the stuff that I need, or read a section here-and-there. Of course, you want everyone to read your book, but the reality is, few people will. You might think that this means it doesn't matter what you write or how you present it. On the contrary!

DON'T STOP WRITING

As I mentioned earlier, writing your book is just one piece of the authorship puzzle. For those of you who haven't finished writing, or for those starting a new project, once you start writing, don't stop! Keep writing until you're done. Set – and stick to – a schedule that is realistic and manageable for you. If you decide, "okay, I'm going to write for five hours a week," adhere to that schedule and keep the momentum going. Persistence and patience are key: if you take a break for too long, it's even harder to get back in the swing of things. Some writers abandon projects when they aren't in the right state of mind. If you slow down or stop now, it will take you even longer to finish!

FORMATTING

Think of what kind of book you're writing. It could be a novel, a self-help book, a biography or a non-fiction work. The type of book you're writing will govern your design and its effect on your readers.

The formatting of your book is just as important as the content. Bullet points, images and subheadings can add visual appeal and keep things organized. Q&A's, infographics, and coherent design catch readers' attention by highlighting your most important points.

TESTIMONIALS

How often do you check Amazon, Yelp, or TripAdvisor reviews before making a purchase or trying a new restaurant for dinner? Or see a movie without reading at least one review? We rely on customer reviews and word-of-mouth for a lot of our recreational experiences, and business recommendations are no different. Your book is a chance for you to showcase your skills and experience for future clients, so you cannot publish your book without including some testimonials from members of your community.

Good writers show, rather than tell. It's easy to include your bio that says, "I've done X, Y, Z..." but including testimony from satisfied clients shows that you can put your money where your mouth is. What are people saying about you? About your book? This is important, because your book is your product, and your image as an author is your brand.

How do you get feedback to use as a testimonial if you're just starting out?

It's easy: look to the people you are already helping. Now, you might be thinking, "oh, goodness, Ari, I'm really new to this; I've never helped anybody," but odds are, if you're passionate about your *why* and you know who your target audience is, you're probably already doing something! And if not, you'd better get to it! Let me tell you how.

Say you are a talented seamstress. You may have relatives or friends who ask you to design their dresses or make repairs. This is great! Ask for a testimonial that you can publish. Start charging. Create a business from it, even if it's small in scale, before you bill yourself as an expert. When someone hears about your services and what you can do from another person, it means a lot more than hearing it from you.

I could talk about myself all day. I could talk about my clients' results and my own successes, and I could back it up with figures and examples. But when you hear it from someone who has worked with me, it becomes more believable, because people relate to results and emotions more than rote facts. When a client says, "yeah, I work with Ari, she did my book for me and helped me with my marketing plan, and I was able to make X amount of money," that's better marketing than me putting myself out there.

ENLIST A TEAM OF PUBLISHING PROS

Everyone has different strengths. You might be a great writer or teacher, but do you know how to market your book? Do you know how to effectively sell a story to convert clients? Do you put in offers, schedule events and position yourself as an expert?

If it's your first time writing a book, one of the best pieces of advice I can offer is to work with a publishing company. Of course, you can try to do it all on your own, but it can be overwhelming when you don't know where to start. If I could go back and do one thing differently, I would hire a publishing company to guide me through my first book launch and marketing plan. A publishing team can do a lot of the work for you, giving you a chance to learn from them for future projects. **If you're putting yourself out there as an author for the first time, get some help from people who know the business and can help you get it done right the first time.**

Never compromise when it comes to the quality of your product. Your team is critical right from the beginning. Publishing companies are great because they already have teams of writers, proofreaders, editors, graphic designers and marketing professionals in place. Having access to experts who know what they're doing can give you a huge boost.

I always say that marketing is magic, because you've got to *make it happen.*

I'm not very tech-savvy, and I find myself getting overwhelmed by putting ads and marketing copy together for launch pages, social media profiles, etc. Do you have any recommendations?

Have someone else do it for you! Think of delegating these tasks as an investment in your business; you don't want to waste your time. You waste more time and money trying to figure it out by yourself. Sometimes, when I don't know how to do something, or if I don't have the time to learn something as well as I would like to, I would much rather have someone with experience do it for me. Learn what your strengths are, and focus on what you're good at; build your business by embracing talent. Think of the top CEO's of big corporations: they're not flipping

> burgers or micro-managing teams, they're developing ads and bringing in the money. They're doing what they do best, and they hire other people to do what they do best - even flipping burgers and greeting customers are skills that not everyone has.

INSIDE SHEEO PUBLISHING

I know first-hand how important it is to have a team in place because I've helped dozens of authors to finish their books, launch their businesses and start getting paid through SheEO Publishing, the company that I started. I've done what you want to do, and I want to help you do it, too!

The best way to learn is with guidance from someone who has already done what you want to do successfully. For entrepreneurs, speakers and authors, I host a twelve-month Push Mastermind coaching program, where I become your marketing/business partner. I share all of my amazing strategies, which have been proven to get results. After an initial half-day session to

plan out an individualized marketing strategy, I schedule monthly hour-long phone calls for us to just strategize. The program includes access to a community of other authors who are serious about entrepreneurship, and we all benefit from sharing resources and ideas. We meet four times a year.

Who better than a business coach who runs a publishing company to teach you how to market your book for success? My one-day strategy session can help you to get your marketing plan off the ground and your book launched within six months. I help authors to identify their ideal clients and speak their clients' language. I cover who to reach out to, how to write letters, and what to research on the back end.

When you work with my team at SheEO Publishing, you'll have a ghostwriter, professional editor and designer at your disposal. Whether you need help creating content or just a fresh set of eyes, we go through the outlines and manuscript to revise and tweak, making changes that better position you as an expert. There's a lot of back-and-forth communication between the team and the author – ultimately, all of the changes are approved by you before we go to print. It's your book, and we want it to be to your liking!

Not only will your book look great, I'll also provide scripts to enlist affiliates who will help you market your book to their audiences. You have learned so far that good copy can mean the difference between a "yes" and a "no" from a prospective client, so having letters with a proven track record of converting to a "yes" will be extremely helpful. You'll have my letters, you'll have it all. I will even customize a letter for you – all you have to do is send it out to whoever we decide we need to collaborate with. You get a marketing plan, including sales funnel support, an Amazon Best-Seller strategy, and managed social media, meaning that we draft and schedule posts for you. We'll even help you to design a beautiful book cover.

We'll complete revisions until you're ready to publish. You'll also get ten book copies for free, a $200 value. We'll publish hard copy, e-books or both. We'll create a pre-release splash page on the web where people can go to read about the book, see the cover, sign up for email updates and buy the book even before it's available. We'll help you to develop a product – whether it's a service, an educational course or an item for purchase, you'll be well on your way to growing your business. We even launch an email blast campaign for you. Our fee is a steal, especially compared to the $10,000-$40,000 some publishers charge *for ghostwriting services alone.* You can't beat SheEO's deal. We know how to get your book done right the first time from top to bottom, and since each person on our team is great at what they do, we can help our authors to do what they do best instead of struggling to complete tasks they're not equipped for. Whether you're re-releasing an existing title or starting from scratch, having all of these resources and me as your marketing coach/publisher for six months **will show you how to leverage your book and get paid**.

FOUR REASONS TO HIRE A GHOSTWRITER

For anyone who's not sure, a ghostwriter is someone who is hired to write anything that will be specifically credited to someone else. Ghostwriters can work on speeches, pop songs, books and more. When an author contracts with a ghostwriter, the author typically owns the finished material and may copyright it without credit to the ghostwriter. Only the author and ghostwriter know if the ghostwriter wrote the whole book, or just provided consulting services along the way.

It's okay if you need help getting started, or a little extra push toward the finish line. Here are four of the main reasons why people have hired SheEO Publishing to help them ghostwrite their books:

- **Writing a book is a lot of work.** Many would-be authors underestimate how much work writing a book can be. From researching and fact-checking to formatting and proofreading, there are many steps to consider. I have nine people on my staff, including four writers, two editors and a graphic designer. Each team member has a specific role based on what they do best.

- **Writing a book takes a lot of time.** Have you ever spent 15 minutes crafting a 100-word email? Imagine coming up with a 30,000-word book! You can never get your time back, and your family will appreciate spending evenings and weekends with you. Plus, having a pro take care of the writing saves time during the editing and proofing processes. Less back-and-forth means more time to focus on your business.

- **Ghostwriters know their s#!%.** From topical knowledge to competitors' products, ghostwriters are professional writers prepared to cover a variety of subjects. Even a short e-book takes a lot of brain power, and let's face it; you can be a great leader, executive or entrepreneur but lack the skills to finish a book. An experienced ghostwriter provides a better product by supplementing an author's content ideas with creativity, intelligence and new perspective. Professional ghostwriters are familiar with the market; they know who your competitors are, so they know how to set your book apart from the others.

- **Hiring a ghostwriter is cost-effective.** You may be wondering how it could be cost-effective to hire someone to do something you think you could do for free yourself. Well, think of it this way: how much are you earning while you're glued to your desk writing? Ever heard the phrase, "don't quit your day job"? You're missing out on income and growth. Why not pay a professional writer to deliver a high-quality finished product while you keep bringing in the bucks? It's a win-win for everyone.

There's always room for some improvement. If you decide to hire a team of pros, they can guide you through the process with as much (or as little) involvement as you prefer; then you can decide whether you want to learn the system and do it yourself or focus exclusively on marketing and leveraging! **You can contact us anytime by visiting www.SheEOPublishing.com to discuss the opportunity to work with my team**. We'll get your book done right, from cover to cover. You'll have everything you need to succeed, along with a marketing plan tailored specifically to your audience.

◆

BUILD YOUR BRAND & SHARE YOUR STORY

Sharing your story is the best way to connect with an audience, so allow me to tell you a little bit about myself.

While I was operating my dance school, women would ask me, "hey, you know, I want to start my own business, where do I start?" I love entrepreneurship, and I'm an advocate for it because of the freedom that it provides, so it came naturally to me to give people advice on how to start their own businesses and make money. The women in my community were having great success with my advice, so I found myself giving more and more of it. Let me tell you, I was in my element and I loved it!

Right around this time, I was feeling a pull to do something else with my skills. I felt like it was time to use my gifts elsewhere. Running the school was taking up way too much of my time, and it started to feel like work to me. I was responsible for nine employees, with overhead costs of about $13,000 per month. Financially, the business was thriving, but I was never home. I wasn't there for my husband like I should have been; even my child was telling me that I was working too much.

When you have a brick-and-mortar business, it's a lot different from being an author or consultant. You're there a lot. If something goes wrong, you're the one who gets that phone call – and guess what, you have to stop everything you're doing to go take care of business. All in all, it was a great experience. I learned more than I had expected to, and I finally closed it with a plan in place to further my career as a Business Coach.

When I wrote my first book, *Release the Chains*, I had no idea that life was going to change the way it changed for me. People just saw me differently. So many people want to write a book, but don't know how or never get around to it. When they saw that I had done it, it really elevated me in my business and my personal life. It put me head and shoulders above my competitors.

We all face competition, regardless of our career paths or walks of life. Personally, I think competition is a good thing. I like to look at what my competitors are doing so that I can do the direct opposite. From a business standpoint, becoming an author puts you head and shoulders above the others in your field. It adds extraordinary dimension to your business model because it provides opportunities for speaking engagements, publicity events, consultancy, new income and more. **Writing a book positions you as an expert and encourages people to trust you… as long as it's appealing and speaks to the core of your target audience.**

People do business with people; remember, it's all about psychology. How can you get people to know and respect you? For one, you've got to be yourself and be comfortable with being yourself. Being your genuine self will get you much further than pretending to be anybody else – if you want people to buy your books, you've got to be honest with them.

You've got to get readers interested in what your story is. They want to know, "Wow, how did she overcome that? How did she learn how to do that? Man, I love her story. She is such a good mom. I'm inspired by her spirituality. I love that she's not afraid to be who she is. I love that she works with people and helps them."

People do business with people. You can advertise all you want, but if readers don't know who you are as a person, you're not going to sell anything and you're going to struggle forever.

Who are you? You have to find a way to share your story in your book, even if it's not an autobiography. Your readers want to know something about you, and if you've put together a profile on your ideal audience, you already know something about them.

BRIDGING THE GAP

Let's talk about what I like to call the "'A' Story Selling Method" as it relates to effective storytelling, especially in a business setting.

Imagine an upside-down 'A':

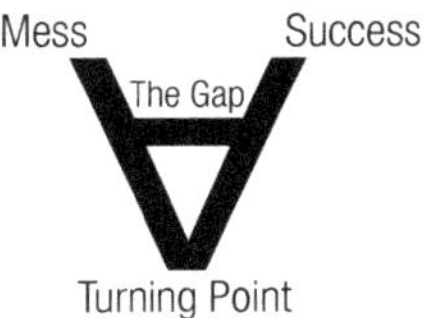

In order to capture and captivate your readers, you want to show them that you were once where they are. They can get to where they want to be, and you can help them to bridge the gap between what you've already done and what they endeavor to do.

My ideal clients are mentally chained; they're prisoners of their own minds. They don't have the necessary tools to sustain themselves as entrepreneurs because they don't have a business plan, enough cash flow, a marketing strategy, or a coach to mentor them.

I was there once. I jumped into the dance school like, "Hey, here I am!" with no plan, no money saved, nothing – I just did it, which it was brave. I encourage that in my clients, too: you can't let anything hold you back, but you've also got to have a plan. You've got to have some strategies.

Needless to say, at first, I didn't. I didn't have a business plan or an outline of my short- and long-term goals, and I missed an opportunity because of it. Somebody liked what I was doing and they wanted to invest $10,000 in my business. I needed it sorely at the time, for marketing, expansion, and to buy new floors. They asked me to show them my business plans, showing what I intended to do with the money... but I didn't have that prepared. That's when I reached another turning point, realizing that not only was I missing opportunities, but I didn't really have a plan or a vision for my success.

During the first few years of running the dance school, we went through a bit of a financial rough patch. The real estate market was crumbling, and the foreclosure rate was at an all-time high. People started cutting back on extra-curricular activities for their kids, and my business suffered because of it. I didn't have an exit plan, and I didn't have a marketing plan to keep my existing customers, either. It took me a long time to realize, "okay, I need to write out a plan."

So that was another turning point: realizing what I needed to do, coming up with a business plan, hiring professional coaches, and working up strategies to better market myself. You've probably had a turning point, too, even if you didn't realize it at the time: whenever you saw that you had to make a change to get from where you were to where you wanted to be, that was a turning point.

Sharing a success story that shows how you got to where you are now **gives your ideal client hope**. It helps them to see that you have the solution to their problem, even if they didn't know it was a problem.

You don't have to do it exactly the same way that I do, but you have to do it. Any time I speak at a conference, teach a course or write a book, I tell my story. Recently, I was speaking in Charlotte, NC, and I only had 20 minutes. I was thinking, "How in the world am I going to tell my story and teach about the things that are holding entrepreneurs back in 20 minutes?" Sometimes, you only have time for one sentence, but if you know how to use your time effectively to share your story, it will be enough to get people to like you – especially your ideal clients. They will know they can trust you; if you know their challenges, you have the solution, and you'll know how to tell your story in a way that shows those ideal clients how much you can help them.

If you haven't examined your *why* or created an ideal client profile, there's no way you can effectively tell your story in a way that converts to sales. The connector in the upside-down 'A' represents you bridging the gap. You have the solution to a problem; you can help your readers get from where they are now to where they want to be. **You have to position yourself, in your book and your marketing, as the solution via storytelling.** Got it?

SHARING IS CARING

How can people tap into you as a human if you don't share parts of yourself? They may not agree with everything you say, but they respect you because they know you. They know how many kids you have even though you're not plastering them on Facebook. They know that you love your spouse. They know that you like to swim or play golf. People have to be able to relate to you. This is what it means to be the face of your brand. **Being an author is like running a business, but you're the CEO *and* the customer service rep.**

Whether I'm working as Ari Squires, Business Coach or the CEO of SheEO, the business keeps coming in because people like working with me, and my team is amazing. These relationships are based on people knowing who I am, hearing my story and trusting me; that trust is what converts these relationships turn into sales.

This is why I don't encourage my clients to attend networking events where people are walking around handing out business cards and engaging in brief conversations. A marketer hates networking events because you are not building relationships there. You can meet cool people, but it's hard to build a relationship at a networking event, surrounded by other conversations and unfamiliar surroundings. It's much easier to influence someone to buy your book or your services if they trust you. How do you establish trust? **By doing what you say you're going to do**. If you signed up for my webinar or bought a pre-sale copy of the book, I promised you a free gift. What if a few months went by and I never sent you your free gift? Would you trust me? No. Consistency and reliability build trust; you can show people that you're serious about your book, your courses, your movie, your movement through your actions.

ONCE MORE, WITH FEELING!

People buy with their hearts, not with their heads. It's mainly women. Men do the same thing, but it's more ego – *how do I look* or *how am I perceived.* Women are more emotional buyers. Have you ever been stressed out and gone shopping, and then you felt better? That's me. I've said, "babe, I've got to go to the mall!". "Why?" "I had a bad day, I'm going to buy a handbag," and he'll be like, "Well, don't go to the Louis Vuitton store."

One of my clients is very new to business, but she's one that takes whatever I give her and boom, just knocks it out the park. I emailed her to say, "hey, I need to see more of you," because even though we had spent time together during a coaching session, I wanted her to start sharing more stories about herself. She was doing everything else right, but it was time to take the next step. I told her, "I need you to do a Facebook Live." She did it, and now she has a life-changing five-figure deal on the table, just because she showed her audience who she was. Amazing stuff has been happening for her since she made that one shift. It might be hard to believe, but something as seemingly insignificant as one video created a future for her business.

Emotional marketing reels clients in. One of my corporate Push Planner® clients, who I met through my *Products That Sell* course, was surprised to learn my story. She said, "I can't believe that you would admit that you've been to jail! Aren't you afraid of people judging you?" I told her, "No, I've moved past it, so other people have to get over it, too. We've all made mistakes; mine are a part of who I am, and my honesty inspires other people to get through their messes. We've all been through something, but maybe my mistakes are different from what yours are." She said, "**Wow, I really admire you for that**. Tell me a little bit more about this Push Planner®; I want to take this to my boss to see if he wants to order 200 of them." They ended up buying 500 Planners last year and 1,000 this year at $60 each. It was all because I wasn't afraid to share my story.

How do I get people to buy my books from my website or Amazon?

Sell them solutions, and be consistent. Those are the big things that people are willing to pay for. Always remember this as you're writing your book and developing your marketing strategy. You look like everybody else, and books are a dime a dozen. Why should readers pick your book? What problem are you going to solve?

My client, Raechel, is a little straight-to-the-point, no chaser. She cusses sometimes; she uses a little humor; she lets her audience into her world. She over-serves, over-delivers, and doesn't have a problem re-creating herself. With my coaching assistance, she's created a tribe of people who know her, so she knows how to get them excited about things that are coming up because *she's* excited about the projects she's working on. You've got to create excitement about your book before you can count on other people to take over and do it for you with word-of-mouth recommendations.

In being an author, as in any business, you also have to form affiliate relationships, connect and meet people in order to generate new income and stay on top of your game. **Your personal brand is all about your story.** Stories are what get you noticed, and better yet, remembered. A good story is the difference between regular and extraordinary. If you think about some of the people that you follow on social media, you might feel like you know them pretty well. You know at least a little bit about them. How much do people know about you? Probably not a lot. This is why you're not making a lot of sales: because people don't know you. Let them get to know you. Show them your world, without bringing them too deep in.

Usually, I don't share much about my husband because he's very private. He's pretty shy, so he doesn't like to do much on social media. Since we've launched our film business together, with me on the forefront and him behind-the-scenes, I'm slowly and strategically planning to use these marketing tools to bring my husband a little bit closer to the spotlight. You'll start to see me speaking of my husband more often because he's a part of my movement and I need him involved in the social media campaigns for something that I have projected for two years from now!

SHOW, DON'T TELL

You now know you want to be top-of-mind, and you know you need a story. Stories create buzz; more buzz means more awareness, which leads to higher top-of-mind positioning. You want people to already be waiting on the day you drop your book, or when you speak at an event. The best way is to create a story.

We see these stories in ad campaigns and commercials all over the place. One of the best examples is Jared from Subway sandwich shops. Whether they planned it strategically or it happened by accident, that was an expert marketing move – I don't know if anyone knew it was going be such a huge success, but it was.

Jared was once a heavyset guy. He ate at Subway every day for a year or so, and he lost more than 200 pounds. In the commercial, Jared is wearing the size 62 pants that used to be his size, and when we see this skinny man with a tangible example of where he used to be, it makes him easier to relate to.

Imagery usually plays on familiarity, and people can identify with a regular guy. We saw who Jared was in those Subway ads. He shared that he was always eating out; he was overeating and not getting enough exercise, and he was overweight and unhappy because of it. Once he started eating Subway sandwiches, he started losing weight. Now he's happy and he's thin and he's smiling while he's eating his sandwich. The story was very simple, and it maximized visuals; you would even walk into a Subway restaurant and see a picture or life-size cardboard cutout of Jared with his big old pants, half their size. When someone thinks, "I'm going to get myself a Subway sandwich because I can be like Jared," it's the story at work. The Jared story helped Subway to grow their US sales to $11.5 billion in 2011, and they expanded to more than 38 thousand locations from that marketing.

Think back to the upside-down 'A' we looked at before. Jared's story starts with where he was; his turning point was eating Subway sandwiches; we see where he is now (skinny) as proof that it worked. The bridging the gap was the correlation of the Subway sandwiches being the answer to his problem. **Don't' forget to surprise and to intrigue people** whenever possible. Don't overdo the hype; some of the best marketing campaigns are successful because they are very minimal.

Your marketing is all about your story. Your story can be motivational, inspiring people with your experiences. Everybody loves a good comeback story; it's a no-brainer to share our stories in our books, but it has to extend to marketing, too. Are readers intrigued by your story before you launch the book, or are you trying to attract readers to your story after you write the book? If a reader is already interested in your story, your novel, your expertise, they'll be a little bit more inclined to buy the book, then book you to speak, book you for media appearances, buy your programs and services, and join your movement.

◆

MARKET FOR SALES

Marketing involves tracking prospects and getting them interested in what you have to sell. Marketing is not about converting interested prospects into paying customers. Marketing is about creating a desire for something people didn't think they needed or wanted in the first place. Finding qualified prospects quickly and inexpensively is both an art and a science.

Since no two books are the same, and no two authors are the same, of course it follows that no two marketing strategies are the same. We all have different reasons for writing our books. When you write your book, the most important thing to consider is *why.* But when you develop your marketing plan, you'll need some more: *who, what, where, when* and *how* in order to make sales and leverage your business. Who can my book help? What else can I offer with my skills? Where is my community? **How do I get people to buy my book?**

Of course, you don't want to look like everybody else who has written a book – you want to stand out in order to be heard over the noise of the market. What makes you unique? What can you do to get noticed? How can your book be the solution to somebody's problem?

FIRST IMPRESSIONS

Want people to buy from you? They're going to want to see some stats.

This is similar to the importance of including testimonials in your book – if you want to position yourself as an expert, you're going to have to prove it. Readers want to see statistics and have real-world situational examples; readers are tired of *not getting anything* from what they're reading, so as an author and a marketer, you want to make sure your book stands out.

They say "don't judge a book by its cover." In real life, no, but when it comes to books, yes. When I go to the bookstore or the library, the cover is what first grabs my attention. Your cover has to match your brand. It has to captivate and magnetize your audience to you. When you post it online, or you share with your community, or when Amazon suggests it, you want it to look good enough that someone who has no idea what you're about would want to check it out. Your cover design should look professional and speak to your ideal audience.

We live in a new era of **extreme marketing**. Sometimes, it can be strategic to plan something over-the-top and out-of-the-blue. Celebrities often engage in forms of extreme marketing – they set up beef, they say and do crazy things, they go to places just to be seen there. **Don't be afraid** to offer a hook. Leverage odd items, old items, different shapes and different sizes.

Everyone wants to know, "what's in it for me?" and you have to be ready to answer directly what is in it for the prospect. Most of the people who are putting out books haven't thought about any of this – they just want to write books; they don't understand what it takes to become an author. That's fine if you're not in business to create income and launch a movement, but we're here to get paid from our books!

You need to master content marketing. Identify and tend to readers' pain points – the things that bother them in their lives – without making them feel bad. Some people are easily offended, but those aren't my ideal clients so I don't care. My ideal clients are people that appreciate that I keep it real; they want me to push on their pain points to help them realize that they could be doing better, but you have to do it in a way that works for your ideal client. Every strategy is different.

You have to **keep your marketing relevant, fresh and interesting**. It creates trust. You have to engage with readers. You have to make sure that your whole brand is packaged correctly.

AMAZON

Marketing, whether it's on your website or in person, can make you or break you. In order to position yourself as an expert, you want your book to gain as much exposure as possible and be available to a wide range of readers. Many of my clients want to become Amazon Best-Selling Authors. Every one of my clients who has expressed an interest in the Amazon Best-Seller program has been able to do it, but no two strategies were the same – even for books by the same author. Every business is different. If it's important to you, you can make it happen, too, but first I'll let you in on a few of the secrets I've learned as a business owner, publisher and author myself.

The first big secret is that **it doesn't take much to become an Amazon Best-Seller**. Anyone can achieve it; even if you just do the bare minimum when it comes to pre-launching and marketing.

The second big secret is that **you shouldn't put your focus on being an Amazon Best-Seller.** Their program doesn't do enough to get you paid. Amazon takes a percentage of your income for each sale, and those people who buy your book from Amazon are *their* customers. This means you don't know who is interested in your book and don't have any information on how to reach them to offer your services and products.

Of course, your mileage may vary. Some people don't care about the percentage that Amazon keeps because they just want to be an Amazon Best-Selling Author. Unfortunately, technically no one at Amazon is working with you. No one is going to pay your more for your products or services because you're an Amazon Best-Selling Author. I hate to burst anyone's bubble, but I have to keep it real: being an Amazon Best-Seller is really not that big of a deal.

Do you know how many sales it takes to become an Amazon Best-Selling Author? **Seven.** That's it. I know from experience: all of my clients who have wanted to be a part of the Best-Seller program have been able to do it by following my advice.

A reader in the general public might see "Amazon Best-Seller" in an author's profile or on the cover of their book and think, "wow, this person is serious." It sounds impressive to the readers who doesn't realize how easy it is to attain, but to authors, publishers, savvy entrepreneurs and others in the industry, it's just not that remarkable.

When I released my second book, *All I See Is Possibility,* the only reason why I launched a marketing campaign focused on Amazon Best-Selling success was to be able to say, "I did it." I knew that if I wanted to teach my clients how to do it, I needed to know how to do it myself. I said, "I'd better just go ahead and go for it," and I put my marketing plan together with the goal of becoming an Amazon Best-Seller. I had already helped other people to do it, and when it was time to put my knowledge to the test, I followed the same advice I'm giving you here. I created a system, and then I followed through on it. It was very easy.

Selling books is important, but I'm interested in making money, and **the real money comes from leveraging your book into continuing business opportunities.** Sure, I sell books online and at speaking engagements; I have contracts with quotas to be met and the extra money is nice, but that's not the money that I'm looking forward to. I'm more interested in using my book as my business card, thinking of my book as leverage to create something major.

So let me tell you what it takes to become an Amazon Best-Selling Author. Are you ready? This is the big secret that people are spending thousands of dollars to learn. **All you have to do is have all of your sales on one day or during one week.** That's it.

Of course, it's not as easy as finishing your book and saying, "okay, buy my book now, it's done," because you absolutely have to get people interested. Reach out to your community and orchestrate a social media campaign. Get people excited! At the very least, they've got to know the date when your book will be released.

When I was releasing my book, I set the date as January 22 and marketed it like crazy. I told everyone that I was doing an online book sale, and even though they could visit my website for info, they couldn't buy the actual book from my website. I created momentum and anticipation. On January 22 when it was time for everyone to buy the book, I shared the Amazon link, and the sales came rolling in.

Everyone loves a gimmick or a free gift! Consider running a promotion. For example: when a customer buys your book, have them email you or post an image to be entered into a drawing to win an event ticket, a discount on services, or something that doesn't cost you anything.

Fundraisers can also drive traffic to your book. Some of my clients have had major success by following this plan:

- **Partner with a non-profit organization.** An affiliate or a group that works closely with your target audience is a good choice.

- **Launch on Amazon first and a personal website later.** You want to drive buyers to Amazon during the fundraiser, but to your own site once the fundraiser is done.

- **Get the word out in your community.** Let your community know that a percentage of the profits from your book will be donated to the non-profit.

When release day comes, you'll be able to make Best-Seller status and do some good in the world.

I've never sold anything, let alone a book! Are you sure I can become an Amazon Best-Selling Author?

Yes! The algorithmic pattern that Amazon uses to calculate Best-Seller status is pretty easy to manipulate. When you list your book on Amazon, you can choose two subcategories that describe your book. This allows you to get very detailed: you might not become the #1 best-seller in a category as broad as 'general fiction,' but you could easily rise to the top of the overlapping subcategories 'Stress Management' and 'Working Moms' since you'll have a high number of sales compared to your competitors in those overlapping subcategories on your launch day.

You don't have to sell hundreds of copies to be an Amazon Best-Selling Author. One of my clients reached Best-Seller status after selling seven books; another took 23. I have no doubt that you can sell at least 23 books in a day if you follow my advice and put some work into your pre-launch marketing. **All it takes is a little planning.**

My book is on Amazon as well as my personal website. How can I get more people to buy from either site?

This is a great question and goes back to what I just mentioned: **planning**. A typical sales strategy is "engage, excite, entice," which is a part of an author's marketing plan. Then, connect and convert is the actual selling. If you want to sell more actual books on either site, people need to know about it through an online marketing and sales strategy that you or an expert will need to create.

Should I have a book signing every time I release a book?

Absolutely! But don't call it or even think about it as just a "book signing". Then people will just come with the mind frame of buying a book and getting it signed. Call it a "celebration," or give the event a catchy name that has some of the words from the product you'll be offering at the event. To leverage this opportunity, advertise the event to your ideal clients, not just friends and family who will come to support you. You want your ideal clients in the room. **I teach on Live Event Success profitability. Learn more about how to host highly profitable book events at www.LiveEventSuccess.biz.**

What's the difference between an Amazon Best-Seller and a New York Times Best-Seller?

There are rarely self-published authors on the New York Times Best-Seller list; typically, you need to be published by a major house and sell 9,000 copies during your first week in order to be eligible. There have been a few exceptions over the years:

- Patrice Washington self-published her book, *Real Money Answers for Every Woman* on Amazon; from there, she made some connections and started presenting to the big publishers. HarperCollins was interested in her whole package – not just the book, but her personal brand, too. They bought the rights and relaunched on a greater scale.
- When Terri McMillan got started, she was unhappy with her small publisher's plan for marketing her debut novel; she soon started selling books from the back of her car and wrote to thousands of African-American bookstores. She funded her own book tour and eventually sold all 5,000 copies of *Mama*, which helped her gain notoriety. Eventually, Terri got picked up by Viking, a publishing division of Penguin Random House, and several of her novels have been adapted for the big screen.

I want to release an e-book, but I'm not sure that I want to do it through Amazon. Is there a way to have my book available for a digital download aside from Amazon's Kindle (.azw) format?

Yes! There are a number of free websites and programs you can use to convert your book to digital format. Here are some of my favorites:

- **Adobe PDF** – Portable Document Files enjoy widespread popularity because they can be opened by a variety of devices, operating systems and programs. There are a ton of programs, plug-ins and sites that will allow you to create a PDF from almost any other file extension. Hosting services (you may already have this if you have a personal website) will let you upload the PDF to their servers, and you can send readers a link to the file, which they can view or save.

- **Calibre E-book Management Software** – this free program allows you to convert Word documents, PDFs and more to a number of e-book formats, including the .AZW file used by Amazon's Kindle.

- **FlippingBook** – this format uses HTML5, which is the standard programming language used to create webpages, for a very visually engaging display that can be embedded directly into your website – the pages even look like they're flipping!

Every book is different; there are definitely pros and cons to having yours available on Amazon. It's not unheard of for companies to only buy books either directly from the publisher or via Amazon. Remember, though, that you don't *have to* be on Amazon to sell – plenty of authors and entertainers don't!

One of the things you miss out on with Amazon is the chance to engage with your readers. Obviously, if somebody is buying your book, they could be a potential client for additional services, but how would you know that when Amazon doesn't tell you who's buying! They don't give you a list of who bought the book and their email addresses, even though they collect that information themselves. It's a shame, because this list would be really valuable to the author.

Selling from your own website means more money in your pocket at the end of the day, especially because it affords the opportunity to connect with your readers. They're already interested, so it's a great way to boost rapport and develop opportunities. For example, I like to reach out to let readers know I've received their orders and provide a tracking number for the package. I can also send personalized recommendations or let them know about events in their area. Amazon doesn't offer any kind of personal touch. Directing readers and clients to your personal website gives them a chance to learn more about you. From there, they can sign up for free offers, future notifications and buy more products. They can join your community. It's all about building your list.

◆

ENGAGE WITH READERS

Being an author is a business, and in order to thrive, **you'll need to build a base of readers and clients who will come back to you again and again.** Communication is a two-way street. You've identified your audience, and you've figured out your personal brand. Now, it's time to use your story and unique skill set to engage thoughtfully with your community. That's what drives sales.

It takes time to establish trust and build relationships. People aren't going to buy from you right away; you have to create a community first. One thing you can do to get the ball rolling is to include free and/or paid offers in connection with your book.

One of my favorite authors, Robert Kawasaki, does this with every one of his projects. Each of his books has something different: he's given away classes, training sessions, CD's, DVD's, and other books.

My client Jerry wanted to publish a book and I was surprised when I received his draft: he didn't make a single offer in his book. He didn't say, "call me for a free consultation," or provide contact info for anyone who would have been interested in booking him for talks or buying his products. My team was able to create *a little bit of marketing magic*; even though he hadn't signed up for a package, as a business coach I just didn't feel right putting his book out there without it. Your book shouldn't be the end of the line: whether it's a free offer, another book, a chance to learn or an opportunity to work with you one-on-one, you've got to keep the interest of your readers.

CLAIM YOUR FREE TICKET!

Remember: people don't always read books, but everyone likes free stuff. At the very beginning of each of my books, there's the cover page, which I sign with a nice little note, and the next page is full of free offers:

"Eleven Free Gifts Inside Just for You"

"Success Kits to Help You Pull Back the Mental Barriers That Prevent Love, Peace and Abundance from Entering Your Life"

"Assessments to See If You Are Ready to Move to a New Level in Life"

"Guide to Becoming More Productive and Reaching for Success"

"Bringing Awareness to Distractions and How You Can Avoid Them"

"Parenting Tips for Breaking Generational Chains"

"One Month to Peace: a 31-Day Devotional" full of scriptures and prayers

What does that do? People may not even read the book but guess what, they got their free gift, and now they're on your email list. Use that email list to send a link to join your social media group. You have to constantly be building the tribe of people who want to buy from you.

LOOK THE PART

Aim at your target audience: your personal brand, your story and your marketing copy should align and present a clear message. Use headlines and subtitles that are going to attract people to you. When you create a flyer or you're sending out emails, the headline should be so enticing that your ideal client can't help but want to get more information. When I started working on *Release That Book and Get Paid,* I paired a professional picture of myself with a title that I knew was going to attract aspiring authors, writers who've released their books but lost money or didn't make any money, and people who need some help in releasing their books and leveraging that into opportunities to get paid.

Appearance isn't everything, but first impressions are crucial. You want your readers to see the *real* you, but you also don't want to show up on Facebook Live looking like a hot mess. It's a balancing act to present your brand as an overall package, and consistency goes a long way. For example, if you're in the fitness niche, make sure that your gear matches. Know your unique selling proposition and how to position yourself as an expert at something, whether it's a product or a skill that you can turn into a service. Happy, friendly and welcoming personal brands naturally attract clients.

BRAINS BEFORE BEAUTY

Of course, you have to have some market knowledge; that's just Business 101. I spend a lot of time working with clients who don't have enough market knowledge. Market knowledge can be industry or topic-specific; not all markets are the same, so not all analyses have the same results. Usually, it's a combination of various aspects of business: competing firms, customers' needs, available products/services and existing financial conditions are all facets to be aware of.

One of the foundational marketing models is AIDA:

- **Awareness** – sometimes "attention" is substituted, but basically, the premise is this: customers have to see your ad. If they don't know about your book or your services, they can't possibly pay you.

- **Interest** – once you have a reader's attention, you have to keep it. This stage is the perfect time to demonstrate how your knowledge will benefit the consumer.

- **Desire** – this is where your story comes in handy: you want readers to hear it and realize, "this person can help me, too!" Get them to see that they want something that only you can offer them.

- **Action** - you have to get people to take action in order to sell more of your books or products, or to get them to invite you to speaking engagements and events where you can share your product and your story with readers who are interested in your topic. That call to action is crucial. How can I sell more books? Well, are you showing readers that your book is the solution to a problem they didn't even realize they had?

Any marketing plan that doesn't take all of these into account is destined to fail.

Marketing is all about emotional triggers, and you want people to remember you. It's okay to use repetition to reinforce the connection. Before you bought this book, maybe you visited my Facebook page. You've probably seen my ad a couple of times. Maybe you watched a video, or went on my website. I'm sure you did some kind of research before you paid your hard-earned money for a webinar or a book. Maybe you attended an event first; it took a little while before you spent some money. That's just something we have to remember as authors and as customers – treat others the way you want to be treated. Don't be offended if it takes a little time for people to warm up to you, and you must not quit.

Personally, if I'm going to a conference or an event, I won't set up a vendor table selling books unless I'm speaking, because no one knows who I am. Now if I'm presenting, I'm definitely there selling books because I've been able to speak and share my story, and now I'll have a chance to engage with people who are interested. If I'm just selling, nobody's buying because they don't know anything about me. It might sound counterintuitive, but do yourself a favor: don't go to these author expos and similar events, especially if you have to pay to be a vendor. It's usually Himselfa waste of time and money, and I don't suggest these types of engagements to any of my clients. You're not going to get paid that way.

BE YOURSELF - EVERYONE ELSE IS ALREADY TAKEN!

Simple messages are important, and a little goes a long way when you find a memorable personal style and stick to it. This is something that a lot of entrepreneurs struggle with: a lot of people try to be like everyone else. When I got started, I was doing things the same way that my business coach was doing them, but eventually I realized that what worked for her didn't always work for me. She had her own way and her own style, and

I had mine. Once I started using the strategies that she taught me and being myself unapologetically, it finally worked!

It's tempting to imitate your idols, but remember: don't try to be Les Brown, don't try to be Oprah, don't try to be Tyler Perry, don't try to be Kevin Hart. My son loves Kevin Hart and even copies his comedy act. I'm trying to teach him that it's okay to look up to someone for guidance, but instead of trying to be more like Kevin Hart, he's got to be himself. What's his style? He's seen enough of Kevin Hart; now it's time to copy his strategy by putting himself out there and creating his own style.

In an impersonal world full of robots, screens and copy-and-pastes, people crave intimate connection more than ever before. People want to be talked to like regular people. **Your personal style is what sets you apart from the competition**, but each audience has its own style, too – what works for my target audience might not work for yours. Figure out what works for you and your audience and stick to it. Be ethical and truthful, too; of course, that's just common sense.

Emotional connection leads to social sharing. One of my favorite examples here is Paulette Leaphart. She walked a thousand miles, from Biloxi, Mississippi to Washington, D.C. in an effort to raise awareness about breast cancer. And she walked topless – after undergoing surgery, Paulette decided to share the stories of her scars with the people she encountered on her journey. This struck an emotional chord with a lot of people. In the back of my mind I was thinking, "I hope she launches a product because she's got everybody watching her."

Too many people miss opportunities because they don't market correctly. Paulette was able to raise awareness and raise funds; she was on TV, but she could have harnessed the momentum to launch and sell a product or services while she was top-of-mind.

On the other side of the emotional spectrum is Dion Jones, the comedian that wears the electrical tape eyebrows. When his Facebook Live videos went viral, I was thinking, "I hope he launches a product around this," since I knew he was already a successful businessman. When he launched his t-shirt line, he was selling those babies out! **Because he**

had a plan. Followers were already asking, "where the t-shirts at, Dion?", but he never mentioned it; he just kept on saying, "I'm coming for y'all." He just kept seeding, even when the interest was already there. This is a strategic move. His videos created a buzz. The emotional connection came from getting people laughing. Once he already had interested clients in the palm of his hand, he launched the product and sold out! That's why social sharing matters.

Profits are ultimately more important than popularity, but **popularity leads to increased social sharing**. You want your marketing to be so good that people are sharing it as readily as they would recommend your book to a friend. Make sure the content about your products and books and services is *good* – high-quality, relatable and clear, just like your book. By targeting your messages to prospects in a manner that motivates them to take action, you'll continue to grow your community and your list. Sharing content with followers who trust and respect you will boost visibility.

SOCIAL MEDIA TIPS

Before you hit 'Post' ask yourself: is this shareable? Your followers respect and trust you. You know your followers and how your specific skill set can help them to solve a problem. Consider whether this post is something that one of your followers might pass on to one of their followers in turn. The more eyes that are on your material, the more likely you are to gain potential clients. What can you do to stand out? Consider the following ideas and exercises:

- **Get people engaged** - brainstorm a list of adjective action words and benefits that you can incorporate into your posts. If you don't know where to start, try looking at posts from peers or competitors for an idea of the market language.

- **Don't say too much** – "less is more."

- **Don't be generic,** especially when you're telling an emotional story. Try to avoid clichés; let your personality shine through.

- **Make your tagline functional**. It's important to be specific, accurate and truthful, but if you can make a memory – something that the prospect will remember after-the-fact – then you have a leg up on the competition. It could be a jingle or a funny saying (Dion's "Is I'm Live?" is a good example); anything that captures the audience's attention.

- **Don't underestimate the power of visuals** – sometimes you've literally got to paint the picture for people: show them how you can help them with photos, images, strong design or a customized logo.

- **Create hashtags** – you can use these across social media platforms to spread the word about your book and your business. Hashtags can be funny, informative, or abbreviated. Each of your books should have its own.

- **Don't be a copycat** – if you do what everybody else is doing, you won't stand out. It sounds simple because it is simple. Everybody is doing Black Friday sales; what about Small Business Saturday? What if you made up your own new slogan for the Sunday after Thanksgiving? Take every chance you can to make your brand your own.

- **Go viral…** - sometimes this is intentional, which takes planning; sometimes it's accidental, like Kimberly "Sweet Brown" Wilkins of "Ain't Nobody Got Time For That" fame. Her interview with a news crew after escaping a fire in an apartment complex has more than 67 million views. There was a song; her lines were on t-shirts; Jimmy Kimmel did a parody sketch. She appeared on *The View.* Instead of avoiding the publicity, she embraced it and she monetized it. She went on to do commercials and cameo appearances in movies like *A Madea Christmas*. You've got to take advantage of this stuff when you can. If you are aiming to go viral, try to connect current events to your business, or what you can do.

- **...but know when to shy away from controversy.** Controversial discussions *can be* good – every once in a while. I try to avoid them, but that's just my brand. One of my clients is always talking about what's going on in the news; she has a great following on Periscope, Facebook and elsewhere. Her controversial opinions are a part of her brand, but **what works for her doesn't work for me.** When Beyoncé dropped her fitness line, Ivy Park, I wrote a blog on my website, AriSquires.com, about the product launch. I related what Bey had done to my business, by showing how people could learn from her product launch campaign and all of the prep work it takes to launch successfully. The post was polarizing, but it got a lot of reads and it got a lot of shares at a time when I needed the exposure.

- **Emotional tear-jerkers are memorable**. So are laughs. Nostalgia, too. However, be careful when bringing charitable stuff into the mix. For some people, it works: my friend Renee set up a foundation in memory of her daughter who passed away, and everything she does is in service of this. On the other hand, I keep my business separate from philanthropic work – there are some volunteering opportunities I'm glad to take, like goal-planning sessions for teenagers that I don't want to be paid for. Kids are not my bread and butter; it's just one of the ways I share my gift.

- **Offer valuable downloadable content** – this can happen in a variety of ways, from offering your book in digital format to creating videos and hosting webinars.

- **Reach out to others in your niche** to see if celebrity bloggers or key influencers are interested in working with you. If you can get popular content creators or respected pros in your field interested in what you're doing, you can get even more people involved in your movement.

These are just a few ideas to get you started. Every author engages with readers differently; I certainly don't have a jingle or a funny saying. I do what works for me, just like you'll do what works for you. It doesn't matter how you get people engaged, as long as you get people talking about you. Personally, I like being talked about, whether it's good or bad. Any press is good press: as long as you've got my name in your mouth, I don't care what you're saying. Since I work hard and share my story honestly, the good outweighs the bad, and I don't let the bad get me down.

If people aren't talking about you, then you're not doing enough. Haters, lurkers and people talking about you behind your back aren't always bad things. Just being a part of the conversation helps you stay ahead of the game.

You can use this to your advantage to get people talking about you in a favorable light. You can even give your readers something specific to say if it fits your plan and furthers your personal brand. It's all up to you, based on the ideal audience you have cultivated. When I launched the Push Planner®, I created a great marketing campaign. Whenever I send out a book or a Planner, I write a little note to say, "Thank you so much for buying this [book]. I'm trying to spread the word about [X, Y, and Z], would you please take a picture of yourself with it and tag me or use my #[hashtag] on social media?" Guess what this does? **It helps me sell more planners almost every time** with the power of word-of-mouth advertising – the same thing that makes testimonials so powerful. When a happy customer posts a picture with the Push Planner®, somebody else sees the post and says, "I need one of those. Where can I get one? Can you send me the link?" and I further my business with that first customer's help.

Creating – and maintaining – a buzz around your business and your book is all about two-way communication. You've got to communicate with folks and keep them engaged with your work. It takes research and adaptability to stay relevant, and like in any business, **it's all about the customer**, the consumer of your content – not you.

It can be tough to keep this in mind when you're trying to strategically share parts of yourself. Between your story being on display in your book and in your marketing copy, you might feel a bit vulnerable.

It can be challenging to put yourself out there without knowing how you'll be received or what you'll get in return. But it's not about you. It's about the people you serve. **Loyalty and trust matter**, especially when you are building the relationships that will form a community and launch a movement. Talking to your target audience as directly as possible improves visibility and reputation. So much of business is about relationships, and in the social media era, it's easier than ever to engage directly with an audience of interested consumers who value your expertise.

How often should I post on social media?

Every day if you can. Three times a day if you want. It also depends on the platform: ten Tweets in a day is a lot easier than ten high-quality Instagram photos or ten Facebook Live appearances. Only you have the answer to this; there's no single right or wrong answer. Do what works for you. Creating magic and getting noticed is a result of tenacity, a light-hearted attitude and camera presence. As the old saying goes, give the people what they want! Warmth and personality. You don't have to overdo it to have a good camera presence, but you should let people see you once in a while in photos, videos and pre-recorded clips you're putting up. Step outside of your comfort zone. You might be nervous because everybody's doing it, and they might seem like social media experts compared to you. Everyone starts somewhere, and no one can do it like you! Give it a try; the results will surprise you.

Facebook Live is not for me. Are there any alternatives that would allow me to send recorded and edited videos to my followers?

With all the video hosting sites out there, plenty of options are available for authors who want a little more control and functionality. Instant Teleseminar is a good one. Another is Zoom; their free membership allows you to record video, and you can host meetings for groups of up to 100 participants. This allows you to get creative with pre-recorded audio and webinar training sessions. You can schedule a conference or event, collect sign-ups and payments and set the recording to auto-play. For those who want a bit of extra privacy, upload to Vimeo: one of their security options ensures that your video isn't displayed publicly, and the only visitors who can view the video are those with the link. YouTube offers a similar setting, but videos are indexed for search and made public by default.

Give folks something to talk about. Get people excited about spreading your message. Grow a community that shares your passion, and you'll see your business grow with it!

◆

DEVELOP OPPORTUNITIES

Money makes the world go 'round; there's no way to survive without it. We need money to cover the rent, to buy food, and to pay for gas in order to drive to work. We need money to live – otherwise, we wouldn't have to have jobs. Our businesses need money to survive, too. We have to release the chain of thinking that it's not all about the money, because it is.

My marketing tactics are more aggressive than others' because I'm constantly looking for the fastest way to the cash. **What's the quickest way we can get paid?** My clients see that right away, and you can tell when you read their testimonies – my system works for me and for them. It will work for you, too.

It's a common misconception that you can't help people **and** get paid for it. Churches are making trillions; the medical and health & wellness industries are thriving; there are rewards to be had for pursuing your purpose, your message, your ministry, or your movement and making the world a better place. You've got to get out of the mindset that you shouldn't be paid for it. You can inspire people and do philanthropic work, as long as you know how to separate the philanthropy from your business.

If you're going to make it as an author, you have to think of your book as *more than just a book.* Your book is more than a product to sell for a few dollars; it's a chance to help others, and to help yourself by creating new business opportunities.

One of the projects I created, *No More Chains,* is an anthology of eleven stories of chain-breaking transformations that inspire readers to take action. Now, we've launched a film from the book. What started as a little $20 book has helped me to grow a six-figure business, **but there's no way I could have done it just by selling books alone**.

Many opportunities present themselves to those who are willing to view 'becoming an author' as 'launching a business.' Whether you're already published or just aspiring, it's about more than selling books. Here are some things you can do to further your career and business as an author:

- **Speaking engagements** – classes, training sessions, workshops … there are as many options as there are authors.
- **Blog posts** on your own site or as a guest on others that share your target audience. Both are great ways to demonstrate your expertise and tell your story.
- **Joint ventures –** working with other pros or partnering with organizations to market each other's' products.
- The possibilities are endless. Few people make it as far as finishing their books, so give yourself a pat on the back for getting to this point. Now it's time to turn your finished book into future business.

NON-PROFIT DOESN'T MEAN NOT PROFITABLE

Before I get too far into developing opportunities around your book, I want to clear up another common misconception, this time about non-profit organizations. Working for or partnering with a non-profit organization doesn't mean there's no money in it for you. On the contrary: most have paid staff members. For example, Gail McGovern, the CEO of the American Red Cross earns a base salary of $500,000 (which is substantially more than the President of the United States makes). That's pocket change for a company with an annual revenue of $3 billion. The main goal of any NPO is to further a social objective; profits from these businesses are used for this purpose, rather than being distributed to a small group of owners or shareholders as in a traditional profit-based company. You can help those in need to better themselves and get paid for it – you don't have to choose one or the other. Local, state and federal government-sponsored organizations can write some pretty big checks in order to have you come in to sell your book, offer your services, and share your courses and training with the people that you serve. It also creates back-of-the-room sales.

What are back-of-the-room-sales? If you're speaking at a conference or seminar and you're selling something from a table or booth, those are back-of-the-room sales.

TEACH WHAT YOU KNOW

As a business development consultant, a business owner and a publisher, it bothers me to my core to hear of so-called "business coaches" jumping in to the arena without ever operating their own successful companies. Their only business is coaching people. Why would anyone trust a business coach who doesn't know how to write a business plan? How can you teach someone something that you've had no success at? Think back to our upside-down 'A': where were you before? What was your turning point? Can you tell me your success story? I know from first-hand experience since I reached a few turning points of my own; these occasions helped me to understand the importance of putting together a strategy to do it successfully. **I turned my business around because I put a plan together!**

My goal is to help you shift your way of thinking. I want you to think and function as a business. This means that everything you do must be strategic because you have a *why*. Know what you want, and know how to get it. Everything that you do, do it because you have that *why* at the end of the road.

Let's say that you were facing a domestic violence situation, and you had to get tough. You realize that your mate will continue to hurt you. You realize that your children are suffering. You start to open some channels of communication by talking to your children, or reaching out to family and friends or organizations to help you. You start relying on your community to support you. You go to church, you keep reading your Bible. Whatever steps you take, this is what you can teach people how to do. These are the steps to include as talking points in courses and packages. You are an expert because you've been-there-done-that and lived to tell about it.

Okay, back to our hypothetical situation. After overcoming the domestic violence, let's say you decide to write a book that will help others who are in a position similar to the one you were in. Someone reads your book or sees your copy because you're marketing aggressively and you've positioned it correctly. They work with women to promote mental health and they want to partner with you. Now you can create joint ventures and continue to promote a movement that empowers women, working with non-profits or for-profit corporations. You can go on TV or radio shows or write blog posts. You can host Q&A sessions or teach classes. However you go about it, you're using your story to engage with readers well beyond the pages of your book. You're showing them how your expertise can make their lives better.

Your success story isn't a success story if you've never actually done the thing. How can you teach something you don't know? You might want to think about working with clients for free or at a discount. This is the only time that I would ever suggest working for people for free. By giving away your services as you're getting started, you can make sure that everything works before the stakes are too high.

Q&A: LEVERAGE

When I released my first book in 2015, I didn't have a plan to form a movement, it just happened accidentally as a result of the book, which is great! I turned it into a workshop and presented to a couple of non-profits. Now, I've created my signature program and gained four new clients. How do I relaunch an expanded version to maximize sales?

I had a client who had already released his book and was scheduled to appear on The Word Network. It was the perfect time for a re-launch – the re-release of an updated version. **We came up with a brand-new marketing campaign**, which was successful because we took an opportunity that came out of nowhere and turned it into a chance to create something more. When he went on television, we announced the re-launch; that same day, he became an Amazon Best Seller. People who heard about it were inspired, because he had already done something that so many of them want to do but don't know how just by writing the book in the first place.

I'm passionate about sharing these steps because I wish I'd known some of this stuff earlier. I've been an entrepreneur for more than seventeen years, and I've had to learn a lot of things on my own, but having mentors and coaches taught me more than just business acumen: I've been exposed to new perspectives, new mediums and new opportunities to make money. Now that I'm starting a film company, I'm exploring unfamiliar territory, even though I'm familiar with the source material because I created it. It's incredibly valuable to be able to tap into my community of friends and friends-of-friends for information whenever I can. I love to learn new things whenever I can; I'm always looking for chances to become a student. Who better to learn from than those who have already done it among the people who I know, who know me, and who will support my work because they appreciate my success? Good businesses and entrepreneurs invest in themselves, and I love to see them create marketing magic.

I want to sell my book in stores. How do I establish a relationship with Barnes and Noble or other companies to get my book on the shelves?

It's very easy: just go to your local Barnes and Noble and set an appointment to talk with somebody. If you've registered for an ISBN number, that's really all there is to it. That doesn't guarantee that they're going to accept you, however; most of the books that are sold by Barnes and Noble are published by the major houses.

One good way to bolster your sales and your likelihood of getting picked up by the store is to set up a book signing in-store. As long as you know how to market the live event - and you do, thanks to this guide! - you'll be able to drive traffic and book sales. This puts you in a good position if you need to renegotiate after showing that there's enough of an interest in your local market that it's worth stocking your book in the store. Costco and Walmart offer similar platforms; Walmart even allows online sales.

Independent book stores are a great choice for new or self-published authors. Christian book stores, specialty shops in your field and local businesses are more flexible than the big-box chains, and most understand the value in creating relationships with local authors that will host events and boost sales. With a great cover, a solid pitch and a personal touch that makes it your own, you're more likely to impress the person responsible for deciding what books to stock.

My second book is complete. How do I launch seminars, courses or workshops from my book?

I could write a whole book on this alone! A lot of the time I spend one-on-one with the authors who work with me is devoted to figuring this out, and again, there's no one-size-fits-all approach. Hopefully some of the ideas covered in this guide have helped you understand how to create a movement and a marketing strategy to match. Start by cultivating a wide base of social media followers – this gives you practice engaging with readers and putting yourself out there in posts and videos. Choose a chapter or step from your book to focus on, and work on developing the ideas as fully as possible into a program that you feel comfortable talking about. The most important things to remember when hosting live events are:

1. get butts in seats;
2. keep your expenses low; and
3. be consistent.

AFFILIATE MARKETING

People do business with people; the emotional connection that builds a relationship of trust is everything. This applies to selling your book as well as to developing the opportunities that will get you paid. This is how you sell more books, and trust me; it's not as easy as I'm going to make it sound. It takes a lot of hard work, but once you learn how to do it, it gets easier every time.

What is affiliate marketing?

A lot of the people who have heard of affiliates and partnerships in a marketing sense haven't tapped into it or utilized these tools to grow their businesses. An affiliate is someone that helps you make more sales. Affiliate marketing involves partnering with others to sell your products and services together. I built SheEO Publishing from the ground up by utilizing affiliates, so I know it takes some finesse to put together a system that leads to the right ones.

The goal of any affiliate relationship is that it will be profitable for both parties. Any time that I can partner with a business or another entrepreneur to boost sales and promote both of our services, I'm happy to take it. At my annual *Pack, Promote and Profit* seminar in Tyson's Corner, Virginia, I partner with Chantelle Cotton to teach the course and sell both of our products.

It takes diligence and patience to find affiliates to link up with, just as when finding clients among your ideal audience. No one can go it alone: we need people who know people in order to keep selling books. When setting up affiliate relationships, make sure it works for you *and* for them. How? Make sure your sales letter positions you as an expert but more importantly, show potential partners what's in it for them. At the end of the day, that's all people care about.

You, your clients and everyone that's buying your book are all wondering, "what's in it for me?", and as long as you have practiced speaking your audience's language, the answers should be clear. You have to know how to say all of the right things, the things that will get you a "yes." Some of it is scripting. A lot of it is research. A lot of it is good marketing, too. But none of it's possible without knowing your ideal client.

I have an aunt who lives in Wisconsin, and she's been working in the regional jail system for a long time. She founded a national association and knows "who's who" on more than just a local level. One of my clients works with children whose parents are incarcerated, so I hooked her up with my aunt! We put together a killer script using the letters and dos-and-don'ts I've amassed over the years from my "vault". My client is about to land a great deal that will elevate her business because of it. **If you'd like to purchase my affiliate letters, template and sales script vault, visit www.ArisVault.biz to see what's in it.**

I take a pretty hard line when it comes to negotiating my own affiliate relationships; I tend to make mine more favorable to depending on live events to drive sales. What works for me might not work for you. In my case, I've spent thousands of dollars to build my tribe and get them to come and see me speak or attend my courses – I don't want someone else to waltz in and make all the money. My affiliates might make more money than I do on commission, but guess what? It's worth it for me because **I want my affiliates to be long term partners and I know money talks and bullshit walks**. At the end of the day, I'm still the one who takes the calls, prints the Planners and sends the shipments. Sure, it costs money to do all of this, but I don't mind because I know how to market and I know how to make money, even in my sleep! My affiliates and clients know I know it, and that's why they're eager to work with me.

Last month, at a conference in Charlotte, I was checking my emails just before I went up to speak. I'd received a $986.00 deposit from affiliate sales. Once I'd set everything up, I didn't have to lift a finger and I made nearly a thousand dollars off of my Push Planner® in one night. Time to treat myself to a shopping trip! Who couldn't use an extra $1,000?!

Sadly, too many authors aren't developing affiliate relationships because they don't know how to, or they've heard about it but they don't know how to create affiliate relationships that **work for them.** Affiliate relationships have given me access to people I've never had contact with before. All I know about them is that they bought my product, but that's enough to start with. It's now my responsibility to build and nurture a relationship with them for future sales and profits.

Any time someone buys a planner, they automatically get added to my email list and they start receiving periodical blasts: here's a free book, here's a discount offer, here's my free 7-day video course, here's a guide on how to design and market your book. I host events and send out invites to the list so that they can attend my courses, open houses and conferences in order to further engage. Now, I didn't know these folks at first. They might not be my ideal clients, but they are clients nonetheless, and I didn't have to change my story or my brand in order to get their business. They want to work with me because they know that I can help them achieve success.

As you grow as an author, you'll be able to take on bigger books, larger events and more serious sales. Coordinate with affiliates to make sure that everyone announces the launch at the same time. A bigger buzz means more sales, and more visibility means future business. But how do you get people to say "yes" to working with you? You have to speak their language. I've had people reach out to me to create partnerships, but sometimes they're not saying the right things. They're too focused on themselves, and if I don't know what's in it for me, it's not a win-win.

There's a ton of money to be made in affiliate marketing. The sky is the limit!

How can I make the most of a potential connection with someone in my field who is way ahead of me in the game? We connected over my book, and I think that she could help me to build a wider audience.

Definitely reach out to them, but before you do, make sure you know what you are going to bring to the table. If you think that this person can help you to accomplish a particular goal, use that as the starting point for your plan. Plenty of people have told me that they want to work with me, but they expect me to figure out how, which is nearly impossible when I don't know the person, their *why* or their business objectives. I'm wary of people who say, "hey, I just wanted to see how we can work together," because they want me to do the work for them instead of with them. Now, if someone approaches me with an idea to pursue, an outlined financial plan and a discussion of what we can each offer each other, that's a different story – I'm more inclined to listen to people who are serious about furthering their businesses, especially if it can further my own at the same time. Keep this in mind before making your pitch.

Who would be an ideal affiliate for my business?

Because your goal is to keep people talking and get the word out to as many people as possible, look for potential affiliates with large followings of your ideal clients. Be sure that any potential affiliate is somebody who already engages with the same people that you do. **Someone who is already working with your target audience is an ideal affiliate.** It helps to narrow down your target audience as specifically as possible when looking for partners. For example, say your book is geared toward teen moms. Are they teen moms who are college? Are they teen moms who want to become entrepreneurs or develop a particular skill? Health centers, local academic institutions or charitable organizations might be the place to find the subset of teen moms who would benefit the most from the knowledge in your book. It's crucial to spend some time doing your research. This time invested in your future is well spent.

Marketing is all about motivating customers and prospects to take action, and it's no different when you bring in a partner. You still want to talk directly to your target audience. This is why you have to know what their core challenges are and how you're the solution to the problem even before you write your book. You want to reveal the benefits, not just the features. What are the benefits of your book? When you are pitching your book to a company, be ready to tell them *why* they should buy from you. How can your book make life easier, or make business more efficient? This will help you get into the mindset to sell in bulk.

Help! I want to scale my business as an author, but I don't know what to do. Will I be able to increase my sales?

When I first started selling the Push Planner®, my goal was to sell 50,000 planners. This was overwhelming to say the least: that's a minimum of 50,000 people I would have had to reach out to individually. That's a lot of time and money invested on my part. Why not reach out to an organization with a staff of 100 people that each require a planner? **500 sales of 100 planners is a lot more realistic than 50,000 single sales**. Now, I'm making sales for 1,000 at a time because I've started approaching even larger companies. Whether you're an author or a traditional brick-and-mortar small business owner, when it comes to these kinds of things, you cannot focus on selling just to one person. Dream big, even if you have to start with baby steps!

When should I start reaching out to potential affiliates or partners?

Right now! It's all about relationship-building, and if you're smart, it starts before you even start writing your book. The sooner you send out letters and messages, the better.

Breaking into the film industry has reminded me of how important this is, even though it's something that I've been doing for a long time. I like to think I'm a natural when it comes to marketing, but sometimes the entertainment biz can be a dirty ballgame – people say they want to help you, but they always want something in return!

One of the creators I admire is Paul C. Brunson. He's been through some ups-and-downs, but he's grown a successful business as an author, matchmaker and public speaker. One of his companies sold for $1 million, and he's a co-host on Oprah's OWN Network. He's a great man, and he really knows his stuff. When I asked for his advice, Paul told me, "Don't wait until the film is done, start selling it, start positioning it to the distributors now." I was surprised because it's not finished, but then it all clicked: it's the same thing I've been helping my clients to do with their books; it just makes sense!

Ari, this seems like a lot! On top of writing my book, I have to stay on top of speaking engagements, social media posts and taking care of the administrative tasks, too. How do you keep track of it all?

Writing out a strategic marketing calendar will help you to stay on top of the seemingly endless to-do list. I used to struggle with this, but the Push Planner® has helped me tremendously, saving me a ton of time and sanity. You can purchase yours from www.SheEOPublishing.com. The back of the Planner features a social media calendar with a weekly breakdown for tasks and posts. On one side, I list the emails that are going out. I also write out ideas for the Facebook posts I want to focus on during that week. I schedule offline marketing tactics, marketing stuff and any other happenings for that week. Some things are firm because they're time-sensitive: a caption that says, "I traded in my Saturdays for success" is a late-night post about grinding over the weekend, and it doesn't have the same impact if I post it on a Monday. Some things can be moved around: I draft email newsletters to send out throughout the week and stream on Facebook Live and Instagram stories to share things like a preview of the cover of my latest book. I send out postcards by mail and communicate with followers on LinkedIn. These things are stickied so that if I need to move them around, I can. Maybe the postcards haven't arrived from the printer, or a newsworthy event makes a certain post more or less timely. This system allows me to see what *has to* get done right away and what offers some wiggle room. I can manage my time because I have a clear picture of everything that's happening with my business, all in one place. I can create a bigger buzz and reach a more ideal audience because I constantly seed interest in my work by posting across a variety of platforms. This is what it takes to be successful.

Leverage, leverage, leverage. Your book is your business card. If you think about it that way, then you'll shift your mindset away from being a "writer" and toward being an "author" with a plan for success and a path for career development! Books get people talking – from the Bible to Shakespeare and throughout civilized history, their stories and ideas have been the force driving communities, cultures and revolutionary movements to make the changes we want to see in our world. Writing your book is just the beginning: products, programs and services related to your book will generate additional streams of revenue. Courses and speaking engagements allow you to make money, boost sales and gain exposure as a top member of your field. Stay involved in the community of readers you cultivate: they are the ones who will benefit from your expertise, and they are more likely to do business with you when they know and trust you. Use your personal brand and your unique knowledge to position yourself as an expert and **get paid**.

Tag me @arisquires, @arisquiresspeaks or use #ReleaseThatBook to let me know how these tips are working for you, and I'll send you a free gift!

◆

YOU ARE AMAZING!

CONGRATULATIONS!

I'M SO PROUD OF YOU! YOU DID IT!

It is time for you to shine your light and to show the world who you are. Take on board everything you have learned or gotten reacquainted with and step forward into the world with new strategies and a new mindset to release that book and get paid!

Re-visit these chapters and tools whenever you feel you need support. Use the exercises, tactics and resources you have learned whenever you need a boost.

Don't make a mistake and forget to visit my website to receive your FREE Gift to ensure you have more proven tools to create a business you love that sets you financially free!
www.FreeGiftFromAri.com

Also follow me on social media.
FB: @arisquiresspeaks
TWITTER: @arisquiresspeak
IG: @arisquiresspeaks

If you have some feedback, or if you would love to share with me what you discovered, I would love to hear from you! Please email me at... **info@arisquires.com**

Congratulations again!

NOTHING WORKS UNLESS YOU DO!

ABOUT ARI SQUIRES

Ari Squires is the founder and SheEO of Profit Attraction Academy, where she has helped clients reach and surpass their profit goals. Her agency has worked with some of the greatest entrepreneurs in personal and business development including people like Paul C. Brunson (OWN Network) and Kevin Harrington (ABC's Shark Tank). The Academy attracts tens of thousands of fans and provides financial success for her clients using problem-solving product creation as well as online and offline marketing strategies.

Her training programs—PUSH Partners and Profit Attraction Academy—have helped students attract tens of thousands of fans, leads, investors, and sales, increasing their ROI through live events, online training, speaking, and coaching.

Ari knows from personal experience that anybody can achieve their business goals and dreams because she is the ultimate success story. Her dreams of financial freedom through entrepreneurship started in the gang-infested streets in Sacramento, California. But some bad decisions led to incarceration then homelessness, leaving Ari with no money and no life. She could only find mediocre employment, which left her unfulfilled.

That's when she started her business and changed her life forever. Today, Ari is debt-free; has thriving businesses, amazing clients, sold-out training seminars, and a dedicated team; and is committed to helping other entrepreneurs build their businesses using her Profit Attraction Methods.

www.AriSquires.com

Ari Squires is the Founder of SheEO Publishing Company, an innovative and forward-thinking publishing, design and ghostwriting company committed to creating polished and rich content books, planners and journals from a variety of imprints led by dedicated editorial and creative design teams that bring great ideas and stories to life. From educational resources, novels, devotionals, self-help, autobiographical, or the SheEO Publishing company signature business PUSH Planner®, SheEO Publishing Company received their reputation by teaching authors how to market and leverage their stories and expertise for life-long profits, media exposure and success.

Ari coaches her clients to have their work seen well beyond their local reach; into several media outlets. "Let's turn your book into a movement." Her premier clients have been booked for local and international television appearances (Trinity Broadcast Network, CBS, Food Network) and national magazine publications reaching millions as leverage to display their expertise and launch their businesses. Her clients have reached Amazon #1 book selling success and have their books in local book stores throughout the country.

As an accomplished business mogul, author, inspirational speaker and film producer, Ari found her literary voice by writing and speaking about her personal story and how ultimate success is simply a matter of releasing ones chains to see all the possibilities. Ari's audience and readers gain valuable insight on how to create winning habits while acquiring the tools needed to stay competitive. She has been celebrated as a prolific messenger and master motivator with an awe-inspiring voice which has propelled her to turn her mess into a movement by use of book publishing and an inspirational film documentary.

Her work has been featured on CBS, Madame Noire, The Black Business Journal and more, showcasing her passion and expertise on business strategy, book leverage and content creation.

Ari challenges aspiring and new authors to live their lives with purpose, bold action and courage. Her focus is on areas of personal development, mindset mastery, life coaching, heart-driven living, success strategies and training. Ari's literary work leaves her audiences with a sense of empowerment and a call to action that encourages them to reach their full potential. She believes that everyone is equipped; people can do and become anything that they put their minds to. Success and money come with discipline and one decision. A decision to live life on your own terms!

In addition, Ari is the author of *Release The Chains – A Woman's Roadmap to Finding the Strength to Reclaim Her Destiny*, *All I See Is Possibility – Wisdom and Inspiration on Getting What YOU Want*, *The Mindset of a SheEO – 7 Core Principles of Creating and Sustaining Profitable Success as a Woman in Business*, and creator of *The PUSH Planner – The Daily Strategic Business Planner Pushing Your Toward Success.*

www.SheEOPublishing.com

CPSIA information can be obtained
at www.ICGtesting.com
Printed in the USA
BVHW040822040119
536998BV00009B/161/P

9 781733 504607